THE STRENGTH TO BECOME WHO YOU ARE

By Carolyn Samuel

SOUTHERN WOMEN PUBLISHING

www.southernwomenpublishing.com

All rights reserved. No part of this publication may be reproduced, distributed, or transmitted in any form or by any means, including photocopying, recording, or other electronic or mechanical methods, without the prior written permission of the publisher, except in the case of brief quotations embodied in critical reviews.

The Strength To Become Who You Are by Carolyn Samuel

Published by Southern Women Publishing

*Edited by LaMonique Mac, The Course Chick,
The Writing Coach*

www.southernwomenpublishing.com

© 2020 Carolyn Samuel

All rights reserved.

No part of this book may be reproduced in any form without permission from the publisher, except as permitted by U.S. copyright law.

DEDICATION

First of all, I want to thank the Lord Jesus Christ for giving me this project, The Strength To Become Who You Are.

This book is dedicated to my husband Michael, my daughter Amber, my son Jermaine and his wife Candyce. A special dedication to my sister Marilyn Jefferson and her husband Kevin Jefferson who are my strongest supporters. Thank you for inspiring me to keep writing.

Thank you to my twin brothers Kelvin and Kalvin Washington.

To my mother, Linda Thomas whom I love, thank you for always being very supportive in my life and in all that I do.

Thank you to my father Elijah Washington who is now deceased.

Thank you to my grandmother, Annie Thomas

who helped raise me in church to be the woman of God that I am today. With the Lord's help and you bringing me up, your influence helped me to stay close with the Lord and to be strong and live holy.

I would also like to dedicate this book to the International Miracle Institute (IMI).

~Carolyn Samuel

ACKNOWLEDGMENTS

You may wonder what inspired me to write this book about the strength to become who you are. Well, it started with me hearing so many people I've met over the years in my life talk about needing strength in *their* own lives.

I was also activated to move with action after knowing God in a clearer way after attending the International Miracle Institute (IMI). As a student at IMI, I have received extraordinary teaching by Dr. Christian and Dr. Robin Harfouche on my Heavenly Identity. Learning about my Heavenly Identity was the first course taught at this amazing ministry institute. This teaching had a huge impact on my life. The Heavenly Identity training helped me to understand more of who I am in Jesus. This ultimately helped strengthen me to bring out the writer inside of me.

I've been blessed to have key people of God to encourage me on to action. One of those key people is my very own Pastor, Hayes Moss. During a sermon one Sunday, Pastor Moss inspired me by saying, "The Holy Ghost can transform you into whatever you need to become."

One day the memory of that very sentence rose up in me and stirred me up. This activated my faith because it assured me that it was going to be God who would help me to become the person, I needed to be in this life I now live in.

I have an older sister, Marilyn Jefferson. She added another level of inspiration to me. Marilyn encouraged me with words of wisdom. She told me I can write this book and many more with the help of God.

Sometimes after being encouraged you just need some confirmation to move forward in what God has placed on your heart to do. That is where the man of God, Pastor Andrew Turner comes in. Pastor Turner spoke a word into my life that I needed to hear to stand up and begin to do what was already inside of me. I needed to hear that word from the Lord, and I received it as confirmation from the man of God on a Friday night.

I thank God I obeyed all the instructions and the confirmations as I began to write this book. I thank God for sending them. It actually gave me the strength to write this book, The Strength to Become Who You Are. God used these people to help put strength back into my own life so that I could pass it on to you.

CONTENTS

The Strength to Become Who You Are

Southern Women Publishing

Copyright

DEDICATION

ACKNOWLEDGMENTS

INTRODUCTION

CHAPTER 1: HAVING GOD'S STRENGTH	1
CHAPTER 2: CONNECTING TO GOD	8
CHAPTER 3: GETTING STRENGTH IN THE LORD	14
CHAPTER 4: STRENGTH TO BE FREE	19
CHAPTER 5: PRAYER, DECLARING, AND DECREEING	22
CHAPTER 6: BIBLE SCRIPTURES AND WRITTEN QUOTES BY CAROLYN SAMUEL	26
CHAPTER 7: IDENTITY AND STRENGTH	52
Sinner's Prayer	57
Poem	59
About the Author	61

INTRODUCTION

The Lord is my strength and my shield; my heart trusts in Him and He helps me. My heart leaps for joy, and with my song I praise Him. The Lord is the strength of His people, a fortress of salvation for His Anointed One. (Psalms 28:7-8 NIV)

Who is strength? **God himself.**

Once upon a time, I needed to rise up to get strength in my own life.

For example, back when I was a senior in high school, I received the difficult news, that I wouldn't get my high school diploma but a certificate of completion (of 12 years) instead.

It took some time, but I did not give up. I talked to the city School Board of Tuscaloosa and I went *back* to school. With the strength and help of God, I received my diploma at the age of 35 years old.

I needed to find the strength to become who God needed for me to be spiritually and physically. See there were times when I got hired on a routine job and was left feeling like I couldn't move up to anything better in life. I would be in fear to step out and put in another application somewhere else with more challenging work but better pay. I didn't understand *then* that God would give me the strength and the ability to do the job.

The concept that God could teach me and give me the strength I needed to become who I needed to be was hidden from me because of people speaking negative words into my life. But one day I heard a man of God preach that God can have the Holy Ghost transform you into whatever you needed to become on the job or spiritually in the Lord. Because our strength of becoming great is in Jesus!

I know you have heard of the saying; knowledge is power. This tells us, (when we understand our strength is in Jesus, and we trust God, at His word), whatever we need to do or become for His glory and His purpose, we can do it.

> *Trust in the Lord with all your heart and lean not on your own understanding; in all your ways acknowledge Him, and He shall direct your paths. (Proverbs 3:5 NKJV)*

One day I was talking to my mother, Linda about how God had the power to lay his life down and take it up again. This made me also think about how that took strength for even the son of God to do.

> *"Therefore My Father loves Me because I lay down My life that I may take it again. No one takes it from Me, but I lay it down of Myself. I have power to lay it down, and I have power to take it again. This command I have received from My Father." (John 10:17-18 NKJV)*

Understand that God has given us the strength to lay things down and the strength to get up out of **whatever** may have us bound. Understand that you can walk in strength and power in the Lord Jesus Christ.

He also brought me up out of a horrible pit, out of the miry clay, and set my feet upon a rock, and established my steps. (Psalms 40:2 NKJV)

We as children of God have the strength of God, to walk in power and blessings. We have the strength and power to become the person God made us to be in this life we live today.

◆ ◆ ◆

In order to receive God's strength, in today's world, we need to have some kind of faith. Little or big faith, the word tells us we can't please God, without faith. **(See Hebrews 11:6)**

We need the God kind of faith. *That* faith involves knowing God is who he says He is and that He's more than able to do what He says He will do. **(See Ephesians 3:20)**

There are **two** things to notice about the God kind of faith.

1. A man believes with his words. It isn't enough just to believe in your heart. In order to get God to work for you, you must believe with your words. **(See Mark 11:23)**

2. We all have something God has promised us. So you must make sure that your faith is strong and unmovable. You must believe as Abraham and Sarah did and stand firm until your **Victory Appears**!
(See Romans 4:17-22)

IF we are going to have the God kind of faith, we need to know what that means so we can develop it.

The key to understanding and developing the God kind of faith is to study how God and Jesus, demonstrated faith. We must first take a look at Mark 11:22-24.

> *So Jesus answered and said to them, "Have faith in God. For assuredly, I say to you, whoever says to this mountain, 'Be removed and be cast into the sea' and does not doubt in his heart, but believes that those things he says will be done, he will have whatever he says. Therefore I say to you, whatever things you ask when you pray, believe that you receive them, and you will have them.*

Jesus was teaching His disciples how to live by faith, specifically how the God kind of faith works and how we should use the God kind of faith.

We **must** walk by faith because without faith in God's word and in believing what He's done we can't please our heavenly father. So we must put our faith into action to live victoriously.

❖ ❖ ❖

Let's talk about victory and how to maintain that victory on a daily basis.

> *The word of God says,* **You are of God, little children, and have overcome them because HE WHO IS IN YOU IS GREATER THAN HE WHO IS IN THE WORLD. (1 John 4:4 NKJV)**

We are children of God living in this world's system and battling the attacks of the devil. It *is* possible to achieve victory over these foes. But these victories can only come through faith in Christ Jesus.

The word of God tells us we know that those who

are born of God do not Sin but the one who was born of God protects them and the evil one does not touch them **(See 1 John 5:18)**

This lets us know that we always win because God will never allow the devil to hurt his children. We can only do this by studying the word of God and praying. The devil takes advantage of those who are spiritually immature and ignorant. **(See 2 Corinthians 2:11)**

Maintain your victory by **knowing** you can do all things through Christ Jesus who strengthens you. We know we can do all things through Christ who strengthens us because it says it in His word. We all **must** believe God's word. **(See Philippians 4:13)**

We have the King of Kings and the Lord of Lords living on the inside of us and there is not anything we cannot do with the help of our heavenly Father in Jesus.

This lets us know that we always win! **This is worth saying this again!** I know we always win because God will never allow the devil to hurt his children!

To be confident in God's love for us and have the boldness to speak this way we must maintain a daily walk with God (through faith and a prayer life). You need to put on the full armor of God so that you can take your stand against the devil's schemes. We can only do this by studying God's word. **(See Ephesians 6:11, and 2 Corinthians 2:11)**

◆ ◆ ◆

You also maintain victory by operating in God's anointing. **Christ is the Anointed One** and He offers us His anointing. The anointing is the burden removing, yolk destroying power of God.

Well in order to cooperate with God's anointing and to be a supernatural proof (providing witness of the resurrection) we must first have the love of God. We must add to that love faith and belief in what God has said. We are called to live by faith.

The word of God tells us the just shall live by faith. **(See Romans 1:17)**

Love is the key to having the anointing and working in the supernatural to free the men and women of God. So if we want to flow in that power we first must love and have faith.

Furthermore, we must know that it's not of us

to do anything within ourselves but it's of God's power and anointing because he's the Anointed One. **(See Isaiah 61:1, Psalms 62:11)**

2 Corinthians 1:21-22, tells us God has anointed us that He has set His seal upon us and He has given us His Spirit in our hearts. We are told we will receive power when the Holy Ghost has come upon us. **(See Acts 1:8)**
We are to become witnesses in the kingdom of God, having "the good news" and moving in the supernatural, healing power of God. All while telling those that are lost, "Jesus loves them, and He will save them."

We know that God is our supernatural source so we must trust God at his word because whatever we need is found in God. All we need to do is have faith in God's word and move with actions that correspond with that faith.

The spirit of the Lord God is upon me because the Lord has anointed me to preach good tidings to the poor. He has sent me to heal the broken-hearted, to proclaim liberty to the captives, and the opening of prisons to those who are bound, to proclaim the acceptable year of the Lord. **(See Isaiah 61:1-2)**

It is imperative that you understand where the

strength to become who you are comes from. God is our **supernatural source**. He is the one person we can rely upon when things have gone wrong in our lives. We must trust Him at his word. We know God can not lie; therefore we can always count on Him. **(See Philippian 4:13, Hebrews 7:25)**

Keeping God's word before us will always bring God's men and women success in whatever endeavor they chose to do. This is because we have that same supernatural, anointing power, working in us all as the children of God.

Therefore **just walk in that supernatural anointing** and watch the power of your faith rise up out of your supernatural spirit (the Holy Ghost). You may be astonished to see the power from on high to heal, to open blind eyes and to make the deaf hear again because you have become like our Father and Jesus, **supernatural!**

Matthew 19:26, lets us know that there is not anything we cannot do if we trust God and walk in His supernatural power, having faith in God.

Let this mindset be in you as you read chapter by chapter and gain **The Strength To Become Who You Are!**

CHAPTER 1: HAVING GOD'S STRENGTH

Gifts, Talents & Skills

It's important that you understand the difference between **gifts, talents, and skills**. Many times we hear those words used interchangeably but they *do have* slightly different meanings.

Gifts are **spiritual** and they are effective through the Holy Spirit. In **1Corinthians 12:8-11**, the bible tells us that the gifts include: word of wisdom, word of knowledge, faith, healing, the working of miracles, prophecy, discerning of spirits, diverse kinds of tongues and the interpretation of tongues. God distributes these gifts as He wills.

There are also special gifts that God has given specifically to help members of the body of Christ. In **Ephesians 4:11,** the word of God tells us that he has given some the gifts to be Apostles, some to be Prophets, some Evangelists; and some Pastors and Teachers.

According to **Ephesians 4:12,** each of *these* gifts are given for the perfecting of the saints, for the work of the ministry and for the edifying of the body of Christ.

<u>**Talents**</u> are <u>**abilities**</u> handed out by God. Abilities are wide-ranging. They can include singing, writing, speaking, athletics, cooking, dancing, art, etc. This is a shortlist of talents, but you get the idea. Talents are handed out by God for <u>His benefit</u> and to achieve <u>His purposes</u>. That's why it's so important not to hide your talents so that you can develop them. We will talk about how you develop your talents, gifts, and skills later in this chapter.

<u>**Skills**</u> are <u>**the mechanics**</u> of *how* you get a task done. It is the step by step procedures that you take to complete an assignment. Skills are developed by applying knowledge over time. Your skills grow with applied use.

I want to talk to you today about life itself and the things people have desired to become. I myself, have become many things in this life: a Singer, a Labtech, a Substitute Teacher, a Gas and Fuel Clerk, a Model, a Housekeeper, and now a Minister of the Lord. All of these gifts, talents, and skills started with me having the strength of God and asking Him to give me the ability to develop in them, while they were yet raw. The more I walked in my gifts, talents, and skills, the better I became in each of these categories.

It is critical that you understand how to stir up the **gifts** of God. It is necessary that you walk in your **talents** to fulfill the purpose God has given you in this life. For you to have maximum effectiveness in both of these it is favorable for you to develop your **skills** and dominate in your field, niche, and zone.

All of these gifts, talents and even skills are developed liberally by spending time with God. I am a living testimony. The more time I spent worshipping God, praising Him, being faithful to His word and putting God first the more my talents, gifts, and skills came to the surface. This is how you stir up the gifts inside you.

These different talents and gifts are in Him.

> *If anyone speaks, let him speak as the oracles of God. If anyone ministers, let him do it as with the ability which God supplies, that in all things God may be glorified through Jesus Christ, to whom belong the glory and dominion forever and ever. Amen. (1Peter 4:11 NKJV)*

See when we are trying to find ourselves, we must know first that we are loved by God Himself. If no one in this world loves you at all, God's arms are always open.

> *For God so loved the world, that He gave His only begotten son, that whosoever believeth in Him should not perish but have everlasting life. (John 3:16 KJV)*

You see through His great love is how you are going to get the strength to become who you are, and the person God created you to be.

The strength to become who you are, **what does that really mean?** You may have been waiting on something or someone to explain to you just what is your special purpose in this life. If you have been searching for your purpose in life, then look no further. I can point you in the right direction.

I want you to take notice of what I am saying, whether your calling is to be a Teacher, Apostle, Prophet, or Pastor, or to work in the medical field, the business field or the social field. The answer to all this comes with finding Jesus. When we know Him, we get to know ourselves in this life. We must always trust God with our lives.

> *(Ephesians 4:11 KJV) And He gave some, apostles; and some, prophets; and some, evangelists; and some, pastors and teachers.} Also see Proverbs 3:5 and Philippians 4:13 for reference.*

We become **everything** in God, in this life we now live in - a Cook, Housekeeper, Nurse, Doctor, Lawyer, Businessman, Police Officer, etc. It is God who gives us the strength to get up to become these bold leaders in this life we now live in today.

Why am I so fixated on talking about strength in this book? You may be wondering if this is a

NEED in **EVERY** person's life? Yes. I can confidently say that *it is* because of the many people I have come into contact with. There are so many people trying to get strength in different areas of their lives. People are searching for strength in their health, mind, emotions, relationships, families, and finances. People are desperately searching for strength in their everyday lives.

Having strength helps us spiritually, mentally and physically bring balance in our mind and body. And when we are balanced this helps give strength in every area of our life to become who God wants us to be. That person who's in need of finding themselves in the time of being discouraged they can find comfort and strength in God.

Strength means the quality or state of being physically strong, it also means power, firmness, soundness, and stability. (**Google Definition**)

Again all of this comes from one person, the Father, Son and Holy Spirit (God, Himself).

God wants to strengthen the person who feels there's no hope or their life is over. God wants to give stability to the person who needs a job to have an income. God wants to heal and strengthen relationships. The person who has a problem in their mind and emotions, He wants to give them soundness so that they can **stand in power in God's strength**.

Seek the Lord and His strength, seek His face continually. (1Chronicles 16:11)

When we seek God, we will not only get the strength we are looking for, we also will have everything else in our life begin to turn around working for our good continually in our home, job, finances and in the lives of our family and friends that we are praying for.

CHAPTER 2: CONNECTING TO GOD

Today, you can hardly turn a corner without finding people who can proudly proclaim their church membership. There are so many men and women of God who have been in churches for 15 plus years, but yet don't understand who they are in Christ. Better yet, they just don't understand how to find the strength of becoming who they are in themselves. Church attendance alone is not enough to know who you are in Christ. The way of becoming who you are is in the cross of Calvary "Yes"!!! It starts at the cross where our Savior Christ Jesus gave His life for our lives.

> *I am the vine, ye are the branches: He that abideth in me, and I in Him, the same bringeth forth much fruit: for without me ye can do nothing. (John 15:5 KJV)*

Jesus Christ is the Anointed One. The name Christ itself means "the anointing." The anointing destroys every yolk which means literal bondage. Unfortunately, people have not been taught about the anointing. The power of God is being denied in some denominations. This removes the power to overcome in their lives because of the lack of teaching on faith. Faith is now, believing is action – you act on anything you actually believe in.

To be fair, some Christians *are* being taught about the power of God and faith, yet they are simply not acting. They are hearers only and not doers. The bible tells us that faith without works is dead. **(See James 2:17)**

That means that you have to put some corresponding actions to what you actually believe.

If we are honest with ourselves and agree with God's word then, we know we can't do anything without God's strength. We need Jesus in our lives. We are looking for a purpose for our lives and that purpose is to bring the Kingdom to the people that are lost and be that witness of the Good News. **(See John 1:14-15)**

Let's be clear you have two purposes in this life.

1. **<u>A spiritual purpose</u>**. As a believer, it is your calling to bring others to the kingdom.

2. **<u>You have a natural calling</u>**. This is the purpose and plan spoken of in **Jeremiah 29:11**. *For I know the thoughts that I think toward you, saith the Lord, thoughts of peace, and not of evil, to give you an expected end.*

You will be *driven* to attain your natural purpose such as being a doctor or lawyer. Whatever drives you, that's what you will be pulled to do but it DOES take **action!**

Knowing our purpose brings about peace in our lives. We use our gifts, talents, and skills to walk in that purpose. If you are out of peace in any area of your life, fulfillment comes with walking in your purpose. You can only find your purpose in God.

God equals peace. These are all chain linked together. We must find the peace we seek in and through God. This is done by spending time with Him to find out who He wants us to become. The strength to become who we are is all found in Him through what He has done at the cross and the plans He has made for us. I tell you God has some very elaborate plans for you. And He will give you the ability to carry out those plans. **Seek Him!**

This is how you begin to get the strength to become who you are in God. Start knowing God. **By knowing God, we know ourselves**, *then* we get the faith we need to believe. The word **believe** means we now can take action of transforming to be great in our walk with Jesus Christ. This is also how you get the faith to be the person God wants and has called you to become in this life.

See God wants to prosper you and the word of God says not to harm you. God doesn't want you down and out, but God wants the blessings to overflow in your life. He wants those blessings to overflow with a hope and a future. That future is the strength to be who God wants you to be.

God wants to give His people a life of blessing, abundance, peace, prosperity, and a joyful peace in the Holy Ghost. This is the meaning of a life overflowing in the strength of God, Himself.

> *For the kingdom of God is not meat and drink but righteousness and peace and joy in the Holy ghost. (Romans 14:17 KJV)*

While you are in the process of finding this strength, sometimes friends and family may not understand your actions or the things you do. They may even misjudge you. As you uncover your real identity in God your very speech will change. When you begin talking to family and friends your mindset will become spiritually directed. Don't be alarmed if people start to not understand your conversation because it is so different than theirs. You no longer think what a natural man or woman would think even in the things you talk about because you now have the mind of Christ.

Another way to define natural thinking is a **carnal mind**. A carnal mind is interested only in the things of the world. A person who thinks with a carnal mind cannot understand spiritual things.

> *But the natural man receiveth, not the things of the Spirit of God: for they are foolishness unto him: neither can he know them, because they are spiritually discerned. (I Corinthians 2:14 KJV)*

The spiritual way of thinking simply doesn't make sense to the natural mind. The natural mind can only understand through the senses.

So don't worry "they" may say you are now crazy.

They may even say, "we can't understand anything about you."

But little do they know for such a time as this, God is working everything out for your good. **(See Romans 8:28, Esther 4:14)**

Your destiny and purpose may not be apparent to them. Once you start getting to know your creator, His vision for your life will become clearer to **you**. It will, however, most likely be difficult for others to understand. That is because God has kept you hidden to make your name great in Him at the appointed time. And in this life, we now live in, only God can make our name great. **(See Genesis 12:2)**

Keep looking to Jesus, which brings your help through this process. He is the author and the finisher of your faith. **(See Hebrews 12:2)**

Your strength is found in the Lord. Your strength has come upon you to become who God wants you to be. God wants you to become great in everything you do in the name of the Lord God.

CHAPTER 3: GETTING STRENGTH IN THE LORD

"The Lord is their strength and He is the saving strength of His anointed."(Psalms 28:8 KJV)

We are continuing our pursuit of getting the strength to become who you are. By now I know that you understand it starts by knowing Jesus. However, did you know that not only do you need to know Jesus, but you need to know who **you are** in Jesus? You also need to know who Jesus called you to be. It's in your DNA to be who God, wants you to become.

*The word of God tells us in (**Isaiah 35:3-6 NIV**) Strengthen the feeble hands, steady the knees that give way, say to those with fearful hearts, Be strong do not fear your*

> *God will come. He will come with vengeance; with divine retribution, He will come to save you.*

Trust God. He is going to give you the strength to be great. The only way true greatness is achieved is through the strength of God to become who you are. We must be who God called us to be and not try to be like anyone else during the process of getting our strength to become. The bible tells us to <u>take on the character of Jesus</u> **not man**.

> *The fruit of the spirit is spelled out in **Galatians 5:22-23** **But the fruit of the Spirit is love, joy, peace, longsuffering, gentleness, goodness, faith, meekness, temperance: against such there is no law.***

Don't set your eyes on a person to imitate them but find **who you are** in Christ.

God is going to strengthen your hands to touch family, friends, even nations. Your life will cause the blessing of God to come to many people. He is also going to cause you to get up with the strength to walk into the doors and places He is sending you to. This will only happen because you are looking to Jesus to help you in every area of your life of getting strength through Him.

Romans 4:17 Tells us we can speak to those things which are not as though they were.

Walk in the strength God has given you. Stand bold in the things of God. Speak to strength. Tell strength to come upon you in Jesus Name Amen.

Thank the Lord we now can command those things to come to us because we understand its not about us but it's all about Jesus. It's all about Jesus and it's all in His strength and power to make us to be the person He wants us to become spiritually.

Think about the word **strength**. When we hear this word, we all may think about someone strong. We often also think about how we have a need to be strong. When we feel we are weak, **God gives us *His strength***.

That way we can boldly profess, "I'm strong in the Lord and in the power of **His might!**"

Becoming strong starts with acknowledging that you desperately need God's help in order to do so. We need God's strength in all that we face and go through in our daily and spiritual lives.

It is very important to have the strength of God in our life because this is what helps every believer to stare in the face of the devil and command with the strength of the Lord to tell cancer, diabetes, HIV, high blood pressure and other illnesses to leave in Jesus' mighty name. It takes strength to obtain God's promise of being healed and to proclaim sickness and disease must leave out of our lives and the lives of other people. This takes strength and faith in who you are in God.

Furthermore, the strength of God is what helps every believer to face every test and trial of the devil and to know that our battles have already been won. **Praise God!** Thank you, Jesus, **It's been won!** Strength is power people.

No one is left out of God's plan. God has strength for everyone. Remember when getting God's strength you can't be like anyone else. But you have to be who God has chosen you to become. There is room in the kingdom of God for you and the unique way you were created.

> *According as he hath chosen us in Him before the foundation of the world, that we should be Holy and without blame before Him in love. (Ephesians 1:4 KJV)*

Let God fill you with His glory and anointing to become who He wants you to be. Let the power of God rest upon you. **Strength *is* power in Jesus.**

CHAPTER 4: STRENGTH TO BE FREE

If the son, therefore, shall make you free, ye shall be free indeed. (John 8:36 KJV)

God wants every believer to be free. This is another reason why we need the strength of becoming who we are in Jesus, the **strength of freedom**. We need freedom not to become who our co-workers are, or our neighbors are or other people; we want to take on the Lord Jesus Christ's character. We want to walk like **Him**, talk like **Him** and do the right things in Jesus. In this life we now live in strength empowers us to do this.

But put on the Lord Jesus Christ and make no provision for the flesh to gratify its desires. (Romans 13:14 NKJV)

By trusting God and believing Him we begin to put on his character. Putting on the character of God makes us grow. Not only do we grow but we grow in God to make us be who we are to be. You are putting on the whole armor of God, which is getting you ready and, in the position, to do what God needs and wants you to do. This brings on that get to living power in the believer's life.

What helps us to walk in the armor? Here's a practical tip: The answer is staying on our knees and faces before the Lord, seeking the kingdom of God, first. Praying always in the Holy Spirit and fasting to be closer to Jesus.

Finding ourselves starts also with letting go of all hurt and pain in our hearts. You have to release bitterness and hate so that you can **get your strength** of becoming who God is calling you to be in this life.

Forgiveness *is* finding freedom. Sometimes I know this can be very hard when others have wronged you but know the best is yet to come. Also ask God, what He wants you to do to bring Him glory. This is when we can run the race of patience.

Therefore we also since we are surrounded

> *by so great a cloud of witnesses let us lay aside every weight and the sin which so easily ensnares us and let us run with endurance the race that is set before us. (Hebrews 12:1 NKJV)*

Women and men of God let's run a race of getting our strength to become who we are in God. Let's do it with a heart that is after God's will so we can give Him glory. That those which are lost will be saved and will know who they are because they met Jesus, through you.

CHAPTER 5: PRAYER, DECLARING, AND DECREEING

In Job 22:28 the word of God says, "Thou shalt also decree a thing, and it shall be established unto thee: and the light shall shine upon thy ways."

This means you can speak a thing over your life, and it will be so. Whatever you decree, however, has to line up with the bible. The following are some decrees that you can declare and establish God's promises over your life.

As you read these scriptures declare and decree that your whole house will be saved, sons and daughters and filled with the Holy Spirit in Jesus' name.

Speak these decrees out loud and with the au-

thority, God in heaven has given you.

Let's get started decreeing and declaring. Let's do it in Jesus' name.

Declare and decree by speaking the following words out loud.

"I declare and decree I am getting my joy and peace back. For the joy of the Lord *IS* my strength and I have peace that surpasses all understanding."

"I declare and decree the strength of becoming who I am in God to be great!"

"I speak life to my spirit, soul, and bones to be strong in the Lord and in the power of **His** might."

Note: While speaking, declaring and decreeing remember to put on the full armor of God.

> *And put on the full armor of God, so that you can make your stand against the devil's schemes. (Ephesians 6:11 NIV)*

Tell that old devil, "It is written that I am going to be great. I am the head and not the tail, above only and not beneath in the name of Jesus."

Declare and decree, "I will not be anything but who God called me to become in Him." (**See Jeremiah 29:11**)

Begin to declare and decree, "I shall not die but live."

Declare and decree, "I shall be great because greater is He (God) in me than he (the devil) in this world."

Decree and declare, "Good is coming in my life. I have good health."

Decree and declare, "I have all the necessary money and all my bills are paid off. I have more than enough in store and bless others in the name of Jesus."

Declare and decree, "I have the strength to become who I am in God. It is happening now in Jesus' name."

Begin to command, **"Strength come upon me now!** In the name of Jesus."

Declare and decree, "I shall find who I am in God, so I can be the best God wants me to be so that I bring glory to God's name."

I will declare: the decree the Lord, hath said unto me, thou art my son; this day have I begotten thee. (Psalms 2:7 KJV) (See Psalms 2:7-12 KJV for further reference)

For I know the plans I have for you, declares the Lord, plans to prosper you and not to harm you, plans to give you hope and a future. (Jeremiah 29:11 NIV)

God is our refuge and strength, a very present help in trouble. (Psalms 46:1 KJV)

CHAPTER 6: BIBLE SCRIPTURES AND WRITTEN QUOTES BY CAROLYN SAMUEL

Psalms 119: 28 NIV My soul is weary with sorrow; strengthen me according to your word.

When we have gone through troubles in our lives and are faced with heartache all we need to do is remember the word of the Lord
 ~Carolyn Samuel

Write 3 things you need God to strengthen in your life.

1._____

2._____

3._____

Galatians 6:9 NIV Let us not become weary in doing good, for at the proper time we will reap a harvest if we do not give up.

Sometimes it seems like in all the good we do there's no return. We feel like God has forgotten how we've helped someone or been faithful in the house of God. But the best is yet to come. Hold on you shall reap your harvest. Remember God owes us nothing, yet He's faithful to His word. ~Carolyn Samuel

Are you weary in well-doing? After learning about The Strength to Become Who You Are, how are you NOW going to overcome?

_____
_____
_____
_____
_____
_____
_____
_____

Isaiah 40:29 NIV He gives strength to the weary and increases the power of the weak.

Sometimes we need the strength to rise to the challenges in our lives. We need the strength to obtain success. God gives us strength when we grow weary and don't know what to do. He gives increase and power when we are weak. God gives us that strength to become great in Him and in our life. ~Carolyn Samuel

Write 5 things you need God to increase in your life.

1._____

2._____

3._____

4._____

5._____

Ephesians 6:10 KJV Finally, my brethren be strong in the Lord, and in the power of His might.

We must build up strength in the Lord, in praying in the Holy Ghost. We must also take off anything that weighs us down so we can stand strong in God's power and strength. ~Carolyn Samuel

Write about how you can build up yourself in the Lord.

Isaiah 40:31 NIV But those who hope in the Lord will renew their strength. They will soar on wings like an eagle; they will run and not grow weary; they will walk and not be faint.

Keep trusting in the name above every name, Jesus. Do this in everything and your strength to soar over problems in your life will be as nothing. ~Carolyn Samuel

Write the things you need to help you learn to wait on God.

_____
_____
_____
_____
_____
_____
_____
_____
_____
_____

> *Isaiah 12:2 KJV Behold God is my salvation; I will trust, and not be afraid: for the Lord, Jehovah is my strength and my son. He also is become my salvation.*

God is our savior and we can trust Him and have no fear. God is our strength. Whatever we face in life today there's nothing too big or too hard for our God to do for us. He's everything we need.
~Carolyn Samuel

How are you going to trust God more?

_____
_____
_____
_____
_____
_____
_____
_____
_____
_____
_____

Mark 12:30 KJV And thou shalt love the Lord thy God with all thy heart and with all thy soul, and with all thy mind and with all thy strength. This is the first commandment.

Love is the key to getting strength. It's also a commandment of God that we do this. If we learn to love like God, then we can be healed, and others will be healed, and others will be set free also.~ Carolyn Samuel

Write yourself a reminder so you can remember how much you have love for people and God.

Philippians 4:13 KJV I can do all things through Christ who strengthens me.

Women and men of God, whatever you need to do, do it in the name of Jesus. Whatever you need to become, God will give you the strength to become because we can do it in the name of the Lord Jesus Christ's strength. ~Carolyn Samuel

Whatever you need God to strengthen you to do write it here.

> **Hebrews 10:38 KJV Now the just shall live by faith but if any man draw back my soul shall have no pleasure in him.**

Faith is the key to getting strength. Faith helps us to stand-up to do what's needed to bring glory to God. God said we shall live by faith. God wants us to walk and talk in faith and don't draw back. Stay in the now. ~Carolyn Samuel

Write down what the word "faith" means to you. Define what it means to walk in that faith.

_____
_____
_____
_____
_____
_____
_____
_____
_____
_____

2 Corinthians 12:9 KJV And He said unto me, My grace is sufficient for thee: for my strength is made perfect in weakness.

Sometimes we feel we don't have the strength to endure because we are at the weakest point of our life. God will help you stand up to whatever you may be facing because God said His strength is made perfect in weakness. ~Carolyn Samuel

Write down 7 things God needs to help you in.

1. _____
2. _____
3. _____
4. _____
5. _____
6. _____
7. _____

Psalms 46:1-3 KJV God is our refuge and strength, a very present help in trouble. Therefore will not we fear, though the earth be removed, and though the mountains be carried into the midst of the sea; Though the waters thereof roar and be troubled, though the mountains shake with the swelling thereof.

The God of Jacob is our refuge. You are never alone. The Lord of host is with us. God is *always* with us. He will never leave you and He's always on time to be your helper. ~Carolyn Samuel

Write why are we never alone.

_____
_____
_____
_____
_____
_____
_____

Psalms 22:19 KJV But be not thou far from me, O'Lord: O' my strength haste thee to help me.

Jesus will help to give you the strength you need. When you feel God is not close and He's far from you, God is just a hand touch away. Call upon Him and God will answer you. ~Carolyn Samuel

Write down 8 things you need God to move on your behalf now!

1._____

2._____

3._____

4._____

5._____

6._____

7._____

8._____

> **Psalms 73:26 KJV My flesh and my heart faileth: but God is the strength of my heart and my portion forever.**

Sometimes we feel we have failed in all we do but we must remember God is always our strength and our portion forever. God continues increasing strength in the believer's life. ~Carolyn Samuel

Write 5 things that have been your portion.

1._____

2._____

3._____

4._____

5._____

1 Chronicles 16:11 KJV Seek the Lord and His strength. Seek His face continually.

We look sometimes for strength in so many places, but we need to seek the Lord's face every day for His strength to be an overcomer and also to be great in God. ~Carolyn Samuel

Write about why you need to seek God's face every day.

> ***Deuteronomy 31:6 KJV** **Be strong and of good courage, fear not, nor be afraid of them: for the Lord thy God, He it is that doth go with thee; He will not fail thee nor forsake thee.***

Sometimes as women and men of God, we fear stepping out because of what other people's opinions are in our lives. However, God's word tells us not to be afraid. Just step into the call or the thing you are purposed to do, because God, has said He's gone before you already. He will not forsake you. God is on your side until the end.

~Carolyn Samuel

Write where you need God to come to meet you.

_____
_____
_____
_____
_____
_____

Exodus 15:2 KJV The Lord is my strength and song, and He is become my salvation. He is my God and I will prepare him a habitation; my father's God and I will exalt him.

Lord, thank you for being my strength and my defense. Lord, I will praise you all the days of my life. I will exalt your name forever.
~Carolyn Samuel

Write where you first met Jesus as your Lord and savior.

_____
_____
_____
_____
_____
_____
_____
_____
_____

> ***Psalms 18:32 KJV It is God that girdeth me with strength and maketh my way perfect.***

Lord I am nothing without you. It is you Lord that gives me the strength to stand and live in safety. ~Carolyn Samuel

Write about a time in your life, where God needed to cover you with strength, and He did.

Isaiah 41:10 KJV Fear thou not, for I am with thee: be not dismayed; for I am thy God: I will strengthen thee yea; I will help thee yea; I will uphold thee with the right hand of my righteousness.

Lord, thank you that you are with me therefore I do not have to fear. Thank you for the strength you have given me when I am going through trials in my life and being my present help when I needed you. Thank you, Lord. ~Carolyn Samuel

Write 5 things that have let you know that God is with you.

1. _____

2. _____

3. _____

4. _____

5. _____

> **Joshua 1:9 KJV Have not I commanded thee? Be strong and of good courage; be not afraid, neither be thou dismayed: for the Lord thy God is with thee whither soever thou goest.**

God is everywhere we go. We are never alone so stay encouraged. ~Carolyn Samuel

Write why you will not be afraid and how you know God is with you.

----

2 Timothy 4:17 KJV Not withstanding the Lord stood with me and strengthen me; that by me the preaching might be fully known, and that all the Gentiles might hear: and I was delivered out of the mouth of the lion.

God will stand with you and strengthen you. The mouth of the lion, God will shut for you. ~Carolyn Samuel

Write down every door in your life that needs to be shut.

_____
_____
_____
_____
_____
_____
_____
_____
_____
_____

Isaiah 52:1 (NIV) Awake, awake Zion, clothe yourself with strength! Put on your garments of splendor, Jerusalem, the Holy City. The uncircumcised and defiled will not enter you again.

2 Chronicles 6:41 (KJV) Now, therefore, arise, O'Lord God, into thy resting place, thou and the ark of thy strength: let thy priests, O'Lord God, be clothed with salvation, and let they saints rejoice in goodness.

In Isaiah 52:1 the word of God, tell us to put strength on. But how do we do this? To put strength on means we don't have to worry about the things of the past. Just get Jesus to be your strength to come out of what's holding you down. When we do this it discourages us from wearing the clothing of shame and dishonor. Take off the weights, lay them at Jesus' feet. (**See Hebrews 12:1**)

What weights do you need to lay at Jesus' feet? Write them down and commit to giving your heavy burdens to Him today!

_____
_____
_____
_____
_____
_____
_____

> **Isaiah 40:29 NIV He gives strength to the weary and increases the power to the weak.**

When lies have been told on you, when promises made from people never came true, when family and friends turn their back on you, and when all seems lost and you are down and out with no money. When you simply don't understand God's plan for your life, I'm here to tell you to **just do it** in Jesus name. Get strength so you can get the power to get living.
 ~Carolyn Samuel

God's word says that you are strong in the Lord and in the power of His might! (**See Ephesians 6:10**)

Declare now, out loud and in writing. "I AM STRONG IN THE LORD AND IN THE POWER OF HIS MIGHT!"

Read this aloud whenever you feel weak.
SPEAK TO THE MOUNTAIN – IT SHALL BE REMOVED!

Philippians 4:19 KJV But my God shall supply all your need according to His riches in glory by Christ Jesus.

This tells us that everything we need is just for the asking of it. I understand everyone will have trials in their lives. But understand that God has already worked it out for our good in spite of the things the enemy uses to try and delay our blessings. I hope whoever reads this book gets the strength you've been looking for in Jesus' name.

Thank God now for supplying all your needs according to His riches in Glory!

_____
_____
_____
_____
_____
_____
_____
_____

CHAPTER 7: IDENTITY AND STRENGTH

During the process of acquiring the strength to become who you are, we must remember this starts with knowing our identity in God Himself. I have learned that my identity is knowing that I have God living on the inside of me. Do you have Jesus on the inside? If so, let this be known to you, that you have the ability to become whatever you need to be.

> *I am crucified with Christ nevertheless I live; yet not I, but Christ liveth in me: and the life which I now live in the flesh I live by the faith of the son of God, who loved me and gave Himself for me. (Galatians 2:20 KJV)*

> *Abide in me and I in you. As the branch cannot bear fruit of itself, except it abide in the vine; no more can ye except ye abide in me. (John 15: 4-5 KJV)*

In Jesus' name amen!

When we get our strength in knowing who we are in Christ Jesus, we will begin understanding God has already given us the power to do His mighty works. This is a word for those of us who have been needing strength to make that move of God.

When needing strength to become who you are, we must never feel condemnation about things we have done or said. Just go to God and ask Him for His forgiveness and God will wash you all over again in His blood.

> *There is therefore now no condemnation to those who are in Christ Jesus who walk not after the flesh but after the Spirit. (Romans 8:1)*

When getting strength we need to make God

first in everything we do. When we do this there's not anything we won't receive from God.

In getting strength in our lives to become who we are, it can sometimes seem like an uphill battle we are fighting. The path to strength gets hard sometimes because some of us have gone through tragedies, things such as devastation, misfortune, misadventure, even setbacks in our lives because of lost love and relationships.

I fully understand that while embarking on this journey you may well be pressing forward against the past. Memories and things that perhaps may have happened in your childhood have hindered you up until now. It's hard to forgive especially when incidents are deep-rooted and trigger us. But we must in order to become who we are. **You can do all things through Christ who strengthens you.**

What if what you are dealing with can't be changed with forgiveness such as deep loss? The loss of mother, father, brother, sister, grandparents, a child or other family members can be devastating.

These things can sometimes cause us to lose hope in the strength to become who we need to be in Jesus in this life we now live. We mourn losses of this magnitude because we really love our families. This is why we need strength in God. We need to ask Him to heal our hearts and minds.

No matter how severe your circumstances have been, it's time to stand up in Jesus. Let Him wash you in His blood. Give Jesus all the hurt and pain and hate you have been feeling or holding and become that son, that daughter, God wants you to become. Let Jesus' love come inside of your heart and heal.

> *The Lord is my shepherd; I shall not want. He maketh me to lie down in green pastures: He leadeth me beside the still waters. He restoreth my soul: He leadeth me in the paths of righteousness for His name's sake. (Psalms 23:1-3)*

God wants to restore His love and strength in our lives and lead us to a life of peace and joy and holiness. An abundant life where we are always having and never without. He wants to give us a life where we know His love **NEVER** fails.

Getting the strength to become who you are begins with you having a dialogue with God. It simply starts with you talking to Him and being open to hear what He has to say.

Recently I have posed the following question to several men and women. "Why have you lost your strength to pray?" Some have said that they have been working too hard. A few said they are in school and too busy. Many said they constantly fall to sleep before they even start praying to the Lord because they are so tired.

Today after reading this book I hope you now see and believe that God restores your soul and gives you the strength to become who you are. It's not because you have necessarily done everything right. It's because of His great love for you.

> *And He said to me, "My grace is sufficient for you, for My strength is made perfect in weakness." Therefore most gladly I will rather boast in my infirmities, that the power of Christ may rest upon me. Therefore I take pleasure in infirmities, in reproaches, in needs, in persecutions, in distresses, for Christ's sake. For when I am weak, then I am strong. (2Corinthians 12:9-10 NKJV)*

SINNER'S PRAYER

For those of you who have not accepted Jesus Christ as Lord and savior, I would like **you to read this word with me**.

The following prayer is the key to obtaining the promises written in this book over your life. I wouldn't dream of leaving you without that opportunity as I end the book, The Strength To Become Who You Are.

> *The word of God says in (Romans 10:9 KJV) That if thou shalt confess with thy mouth the Lord Jesus, and shalt believe in thine heart that God hath raised Him from the dead, thou shalt be saved.*

Now if you believe what God's word says you shall be saved. Repeat this sinner's prayer with me in this book and look for change to come in your life. Get your strength back to get to living.

Lord Jesus, I know I am a sinner. I am in the need of a savior. I have not done everything right, but I come to you after reading Romans 10:9. I now understand I require a savior and now I know His name is Jesus, who died for all my sins.

I believe He died and was raised from the dead so I wouldn't go to hell and that I might live. Lord, I confess it with my mouth, and I ask you to come inside of my heart and life. Make me whole.

Wash me in your blood. Set me apart. Give me a new home. Adopt me into your kingdom as your son (as your daughter). Give me the strength I need to be the person in this life I now live in. In Jesus mighty name amen.

I am saved. I am a new creature and I have strength in Jesus. Glory to God! Strength to become who I am.

Amen.

POEM

Thank you, Lord, for the crown of thorns on your head, that I may have the mind of Christ...

Thank you, Lord, for giving your face as they pulled the hairs from your beard that my face always may shine...

Thank you, Lord, for your hands you gave so that I may lift up Holy hands before you...

Thank you, Lord, for giving your feet so that I walk by faith not by sight and I run a race of patience...

Thank you, Lord, for the spear in your side so I will not backslide from the faith in your name Jesus, because of the power and blood and water shed from your side...

Thank you, Lord, for giving your back with stripes for every one of my sins to be forgiven and all diseases to be washed away…

And most of all the biggest thing on that cross Lord, I thank you for your son Jesus' blood that can heal, deliver, send the devil back to hell and save a multitude of people.

I thank you, Lord, for saving me and washing me from all my sins with your blood Amen.

ABOUT THE AUTHOR

Carolyn Samuel is a Minister of the gospel, a singer and a woman of God, who believes in miracles and deliverance. She has worked in these anointed, prophetic, deliverance gifts of God for more than 18 years.

Carolyn is married to Michael Samuel. She has two children, a son – Jermaine Washington and a daughter, Amber Samuel. She now has a second daughter, Candyce Taylor Washington who is married to her son Jermaine.

Carolyn attributes her perseverance in writing to God first and her older sister Marilyn Jefferson. Marilyn not only inspired her to keep writing but helped to launch her first book, The Strength To Become Who You Are.

www.ingramcontent.com/pod-product-compliance
Lightning Source LLC
Chambersburg PA
CBHW031209090426

42736CB00009B/841